贵州省博物馆藏

瓷器

精品集

主编◎王红光　副主编◎朱良津

执行主编◎唐　艳

广西师范大学出版社
GUANGXI NORMAL UNIVERSITY PRESS

·桂林·

出版统筹　张　明

责任编辑　贾宁宁

责任技编　王增元

美术编辑　徐俊霞　俸萍利

翻　　译　李宏霞　贾宁宁

作品拍摄　陈诗文

图书在版编目（CIP）数据

贵州省博物馆藏瓷器精品集：汉、英 / 王红光主编.
桂林：广西师范大学出版社，2014.12
　ISBN 978-7-5495-6067-7

Ⅰ．①贵… Ⅱ．①王… Ⅲ．①瓷器（考古）－中国－
图集 Ⅳ．①K876.32

中国版本图书馆 CIP 数据核字（2014）第 276575 号

广西师范大学出版社出版发行

（广西桂林市中华路 22 号　邮政编码：541001）
（网址：http://www.bbtpress.com）

出版人：何林夏

全国新华书店经销

广西朗博文化发展有限公司拍摄

广西朗博文化发展有限公司制版

深圳市国际彩印有限公司印刷

（深圳市龙华新区大浪街道华霆路 1 号　邮政编码：518053）

开本：787 mm × 1 092 mm　1/8

印张：18　　　字数：66 千字

2014 年 12 月第 1 版　　　2014 年 12 月第 1 次印刷

定价：398.00 元

如发现印装质量问题，影响阅读，请与印刷厂联系调换。

序　言

历史如河，浩浩而逝，不可泳思。然岁月似浪，披沙沥金之后总能沉淀下一些贝阙珠宫于沧海桑田之间，任世人去凭吊，去追思，去一窥曾经的风华绝代。如此才文明不止，文化不绝。博物馆人的使命便是赤脚行走在历史的沙滩之上，寻拾那些被岁月所沉淀的遗存，抹去时光的斑斑锈渍，让瑰宝重现于世。

贵州省博物馆自1953年筹建至今，一直致力于各种文化遗存的收藏、保管、研究、展示工作，努力让这些带着传统文化因子的物件穿越时光，激活封尘的历史、述说曾经的故事。经半个多世纪的努力，现馆藏数量可观，种类丰富，有标本化石、传世书画、古墓遗存，更有反映地域文化的各类物件，其间不乏稀世之物；举办展览数百场，足迹遍及全省各地及全国各省。珍品纵不时展示，竭力满足公众的文化需求，然观者仍感意犹未尽、叹息不已。为让文化遗产发挥最大的价值，让更多的观者能共享人类文明的珍贵成果，我馆与广西师范大学出版社联手，再三甄选，精心鉴别，最终将一批藏于深宅中的精品文物出版，俾使翰墨丹青，或钟鼓玉器，或青瓷粉彩，或霓裳彩饰，于尺幅书香之间，带着气定神闲的韵致，以精美图片的形式呈现于世人面前，让公众能存留、品鉴、深研，畅浴于人类历史的丰厚文脉之中。

贵州省博物馆

Preface

Like a river, history fades in torrential flows and allows no return. Yet, just as waves wash grains out of sand, time always deposits treasures amid the great changes, inviting people to mourn, to memorize and to peep the unsurpassed elegance and brilliance. It is just for this reason that civilization progresses and culture proceeds. It is the mission of museology devotees to walk barefoot on the beach of history, search and collect the remains deposited by time, sweep away the rusty stains of time, and represent the treasures to the world.

Since its preparation for construction in 1953, Guizhou Provincial Museum has been committed to the collection, safekeeping, research and exhibition of the various kinds of cultural relics, in an effort to make the articles with traditional cultural factors traverse time to activate the dusty history and recount the old story. After half a century's efforts, the museum collections are of considerable number and variable kinds, including specimens and fossils, handed-down paintings, tomb relics, and different sorts of articles which reflect regional culture, with no lack of rare treasures. Guizhou Museum has held hundreds of exhibitions, spreading footprints throughout Guizhou and the other provinces of China. However, even if exhibited from time to time to meet people's demand, treasures still rendering viewers dissatisfied and sign in vain. To give full play to the value of cultural heritages and make more people share the valuable achievements of human civilization, Guizhou Provincial Museum and Guangxi Normal University Press collaborate and finally publish, through meticulous selection and elaborate identification, a batch of exquisite, antique cultural heritages. Different sorts of cultural relics, such as calligraphy and paintings, bells, drums and jade wares, celadon and famille-rose porcelain, splendid decoration, are presented before people in the form of beautiful pictures with an air of quietness, so that more lovers can preserve, appreciate and study them and bathe themselves in the culture of human history.

Guizhou Provincial Museum

前　言

瓷器是我国古代的一项重要发明，在古代手工业中占有重要地位。由于瓷器成本低廉，原料丰富；经过高温烧制后坚固耐用，易于清洗；坯土具有可塑性，可以做成各种形状的器物，便于满足人们各方面的需要；可以变换釉色，或以刻、划、镂、雕、印、贴、堆塑、彩绘等各种技法进行美化，它一经问世就备受人们喜爱，并在日常生活中广泛使用。瓷器从诞生伊始，就既是实用器又是艺术品。千姿百态的造型、瑰丽多变的釉色、绚丽丰富的装饰、缤纷的彩绘和不断改进的工艺，这些人类利用水、火的作用将泥土转变成的瓷器，凝聚着创作者的情感，带着泥土的芬芳，展现着广阔的社会生活画卷。

贵州省博物馆收藏的瓷器主要包括出土瓷器和传世瓷器两部分。出土部分主要是省内历年考古发掘、配合基建发掘、窖藏出土等；传世部分则主要是通过国家调拨、民间征集，以及交换、受捐等形式获得。这些瓷器时间上纵贯汉代至近现代，主要为浙江龙泉窑，福建建窑、德化窑，江西景德镇窑、吉州窑等各地窑口所生产。瓷器风格各具特色，尤以景德镇明清时期产品最为突出。本图册从中遴选出汉代、六朝、唐宋及明清时期的一百余件精品，旨在较为集中地呈现出馆藏瓷器的精粹与多姿。

这些瓷器器型较为丰富，有盘、碗、杯、碟、壶、罐、瓶、尊、炉、笔筒、瓷塑以及冥器等，多方面地展现了瓷器的造型艺术之美。瓷器品类亦包罗万象，有青翠欲滴、致雅静幽的青花瓷，斑斓多姿、缤纷绚丽的颜色釉瓷，自然生动、倍添情趣的彩绘瓷。其中既有朴实雅致的民窑瓷，也有精益求精、华丽高贵的官窑瓷。它们以丰富优美的造型、精良的做工、浑然天成的纹饰图案、浓厚的文化气息，体现出较高的文物价值、历史价值及艺术品位。

其中，部分藏品与贵州历史有着千丝万缕的联系。

"万历丁亥年造，黔府应用"款青花缠枝番莲盖罐（编号33），从底款"黔府应用"来看，此罐与贵州关系紧密。黔宁王沐英，先后征战于川、藏、陕、甘、滇等地，大明王朝近三百年的西南边防，均由沐家镇守。沐英死后，朱元璋追封他为黔宁王，其子沐晟封黔国公世袭爵位，所在府第称为"黔府"。沐氏黔国公的辖地范围不仅包括云南，还包括贵州西部如毕节、威宁、水城、普安、晴隆等广袤土地。沐氏家族曾在这些地方进行过镇压少数民族的活动。沐氏之所以获得"黔国"的封号，正是因为在藩臣镇守的制度上与贵州有着密不可分的关系。器款"万历丁亥"正是第八代黔国公沐昌祚袭位的时间，此罐是这一时期王府在景德镇定做烧造的高档瓷器，其形式应该是"官搭民烧"。它对研究明代后期瓷器工艺、烧造形式以及贵州历史都有着重要的意义。

清代黔籍名宦石赞清家藏御瓷"尘定轩"斗彩山水人物盖碗（编号88），系1976年石赞清的侄孙女石朴捐与我馆的一件珍贵瓷器。据了解，这是同治皇帝的御用品，因同治皇帝重用和赞赏石赞清，遂将其赏赐与他。石赞清无子，将此器转赠给其侄石书林，后传给石赞清侄孙女石朴。盖碗小巧轻盈，所绘的山路、人家、云雾、红叶、老人、童子，构成一幅和谐统一的画面，表现了唐杜牧"停车坐爱枫林晚"的诗词意境。它的精美雅致堪称道光瓷中的精品，可谓当时制瓷工艺水平的代表之作，亦是传世极为稀少的器物。尤其对贵州这个历史上文化相对滞后的地区而言，若不是因为石赞清的关系，恐怕实难能有如此收藏。它作为我馆藏品中传承清晰的珍贵文物，具有重要的历史意义，也为我们了解道光时期景德镇御窑厂瓷器生产的状况提供了实物资料。

此外，图册中收入的瓷器不乏品种名贵、珍稀罕见之物，甚至有的可作为重要的标准器，为学术研究提供参考。

迄今所见颇早的落纪年铭文的瓷器，东汉永元十六年（104年）青瓷罐（编号1），罐身有东汉和帝刘肇"永元十六年"铭文。该罐制于东汉和帝时期，其间流传了两百多年后，却葬于六朝墓葬之中，可见此罐对使用者来说意义非同寻常。更可贵的是，它对研究我国早期瓷器纪年铭文具有重要价值。

青花瓷素以釉下彩的工艺优势和瓷画的美学艺术价值，受到世人的喜爱和珍视。在我馆所藏的青花瓷中，明宣德青花什锦团花碗（编号21），造型优美、构思精巧，胎体上薄下厚，极为稳妥；纹饰系用小笔点画而成，画工精湛、构图疏朗；青花色泽凝重深沉，有铁锈斑；款识笔法遒劲有力、浑厚朴拙，实为明代青花瓷烧制黄金时期的佳品。

明代正统、景泰、天顺三朝，社会动荡不安，外患与内讧相继，瓷器生产处于废弛与懈怠状态。且不见书三朝帝王年号款的官窑瓷器，故陶瓷界曾经一度认为此三朝没有瓷业生产，称之为"空白期"。但从文献记载及不断发现的考古资料来看，此期间都曾经有瓷器烧造，但数量的确极其有限。我馆收藏的青花香草龙纹盘（编号24）作为这个时期的瓷器，尤显珍贵。

全国流传下来的鲜红釉瓷器在各地博物馆均有收藏，而我馆所藏的清康熙仿宣德霁红釉瓷碗（编号49）确实属于这类瓷器中难得的珍品。此品种自明嘉靖失传近两百年后，于康熙时期得以恢复。其色调深红，似暴风雨后晴空中的红霞，浓者釉汁凝厚，釉面密布细小棕眼，如同橘皮；淡者釉面平滑无橘皮纹。我馆所藏的康熙霁红釉瓷碗，无论是造型还是胎、釉，均反映了康熙时期仿明代鲜红釉瓷而又自具的一些特点，展现了这一时期烧制这种瓷器的成果。

又如，造型优美、塑工精湛的东晋青釉堆塑莲瓣纹罐（编号3），朵朵莲瓣生机盎然，恰似盛开的莲花，令人爱怜。南宋时期可与青玉和翡翠媲美的龙泉窑碗、杯、盘（编号16~19），让您品味到青釉瓷艺高峰之作的恬淡纯净。别具一格的宋代吉州窑叶片纹碗（编号11），内底所贴叶片柔和美丽、自然生动，堪称吉州窑中的上乘作品。康熙年间难得的珍品——美人醉柳叶瓶（编号54），清秀雅丽，小巧玲珑，色泽莹美，在浑然一体的红中掺杂点点绿斑，柔和悦目，引人遐思，有着"满身苔点泛于桃花春浪间"的迷人之美……

正所谓"瓷美如花、如花美瓷"，面对如此绚丽缤纷、百卉千葩的瓷器，相信您在鉴赏之余定能获得美的享受。

贵州省博物馆　唐 艳

Foreword

As an important invention of the ancient China, porcelain plays an important role in the ancient handicraft industry. Porcelain features low cost and abundant raw materials. Through high temperature burning, porcelain is sturdy and durable, easy to clean. With plasticity, clays could be made into utensils of various forms and thus meet people's needs in various aspects. Porcelain could also be beautified with the change of glazing color or the application of sorts of techniques such as carving, marking, engraving, sealing, sticking, pasting ornament and colored drawing. For the above reasons, porcelain has been favored by people since it came out and is widely used in people's daily life. Since its birth, porcelain has been served as both daily wares and artwork. Porcelain features varied form, rich glazing color, colorful decoration, gorgeous drawing and improving technique. Porcelain, made from clays under human's utilization of water and fire, condenses craftsmen's affection and carries the fragrance of clay, presenting a wide scroll of social life.

Ceramics collected by Guizhou Provincial Museum are mainly of two kinds: the unearthed and the extant. The unearthed mainly refer to the ceramics unearthed from archaeological excavation, those excavated along with construction and the ones unearthed from hoards. The extant are obtained mainly through national allocation, non-government collection, exchange, philanthropic beneficence and other means. Ranging from Han dynasty till the modern society, the ceramics were mainly produced in Longquan kiln of Zhejiang Province, Jian kiln and Dehua kiln of Fujian Province, Jingdezhen kiln and Jizhou kiln of Jiangxi Province, and other kilns across China. Among the ceramics of varied styles, Jingdezhen ceramics in Ming and Qing dynasties are the most prominent. Over 100 masterpieces from Han dynasty, the Six dynasties, Tang, Song, Ming and Qing dynasties are selected in the picture album, designed to present the quintessence and gorgeousness of the museum ceramic collection.

Boasting plentiful forms, the ceramics involve dish, bowl, cup, tray, kettle, pot, vase, wine vessel, burner, brush pot, porcelain sculpture, funeral objects and other types, presenting in multiple aspects the beauty of porcelain modeling art. Of the varied types of porcelain, there's quiet, graceful blue-and-white porcelain, colorful, magnificent porcelain, and vivid, appealing painted porcelain; there's not merely simple, elegant folk kiln porcelain, but also exquisite, luxuriant imperial kiln porcelain. With graceful modeling, superior craftsmanship, perfect ornamentation and profound cultural atmosphere, the ceramics embody relatively high cultural relics value, historical value and art taste.

Some of the collections have countless ties with the history of Guizhou.

As for the *Blue-and-white covered jar with design of scrolled passion-flowers, and the inscription"made in Year Dinghai, Wanli period, for Qian Mansion"on the base* (No.33), the bottom stamp "for Qian Mansion" shows its connection with Guizhou. Mu Ying, King of Qianning, campaigned in Sichuan, Xizang, Shanxi, Gansu, Yunnan and other places successively. For nearly 300 years of Ming Dynasty, Mu Family had been guarding the southwest border defence. After his death, Mu Ying was conferred by Zhu Yuanzhang the posthumous title King of Qianning, his son Mu Sheng was conferred the hereditary title of nobility Duke of Qian, and their mansion was thus named "Qian Mansion". The regions under the jurisdiction of the title Duke of Qian include not merely Yunnan Province, but also the vast expanses of the western Guizhou Province, including Bijie, Weining, Shuicheng, Pu'an and Qinglong. Mu family once conducted repression activities against the minority groups in these regions. It is just due to its inextricable relation with Guizhou in vassal guard policy that the Mu Family was conferred the title "Qian State". The inscription "Dinghai, Wanli" marked the time when Mu Changzuo, the 8th generation of Duke of Qian, inherited the title. As the top grade palace porcelain burned in Jingdezhen, this ceramic is a kind of "imperial porcelain burned in folk kiln", playing an important role in the study of porcelain technology and manufacture forms in

the late Ming dynasty as well as the research of Guizhou's history.

As a home collection of Shi Zanqing, a renowned Guizhou-born official of Qing dynasty, the imperial *Covered bowl with overglaze constrasting colors (Doucai) of figures and landscape, and a "chendingxuan" mark on the base* (No.88), is a precious ceramic donated by Shi Pu, grandniece of Shi Zanqing, to Guizhou Provincial Museum. As a royal daily ware, it was granted to Shi Zanqing by Emperor Tongzhi out of his trust in and recognition of Shi Zanqing. Since he had no child, Shi Zanqing gave the ceramic to his niece Shi Shulin, who passed it down to Shi Pu. Small and lightweight, the bowl is painted with mountain roads, households, cloud and mist, red leaves, the elders and young kids, which form a harmonious picture and present the artistic conception of the verse "Stopping in my sedan chair in the evening, I sit admiring the maple grove" written by Du Mu of Tang dynasty. Boasting exquisiteness and elegance, the ceramic could be rated not merely as a masterpiece of Daoguang ceramics and a representative work of porcelain manufacture technique of that time, but also a rare ceramic handed down from the ancient times. Were it not for the sake of Shi Zanqing, the masterpiece could hardly be collected, especially for Guizhou, the region relatively backward in historical culture. As a precious cultural relic with clear inheritance collected by Guizhou Provincial Museum, the ceramic is of great historical significance and provides physical information for the study of the porcelain manufacture state of Jingdezhen imperial kiln during Daoguang period.

Besides, of those selected in the picture album, there's no lack of ceramics with rare breeds or extreme values. Some could even be considered as important standard porcelain and provide reference for academic study.

Celadon-glazed jar (No.1) of the sixteenth year of Yongyuan period of Eastern Han dynasty (104) boasts the rarely seen early chronological inscription — "the 16th year of Yongyuan period", the reign title of Liu Zhao, Emperor He of Eastern

Han dynasty. Made in the period of Emperor He of Eastern Han dynasty, the jar had passed down for over 200 years and was then buried in the tomb of the Six dynasties, fully demonstrating its significance for the users. What's more remarkable is its important values for the study of chronological inscription on China's early porcelain.

Blue-and-white porcelain, by virtue of its technique advantages of underglaze color and aesthetic artistic values of porcelain painting, has been favored and treasured by people. Of the museum blue-and-white porcelain collections, *Blue-and-white glazed bowl with design of flowers* (No.21) made in Xuande period of Ming dynasty boasts elegant modeling and ingenious conception. Thin on the top and thick at the bottom, the porcelain body seems quite steady. Applying stippling with small ink, the ornamentation features exquisite painting and spacious composition. The blue flowers feature imposing, deep color and rust traces. The inscription brushwork is powerful, vigorous and simple. All of these make the ceramic a masterpiece of the golden period of blue-and-white porcelain manufacture in Ming dynasty.

Zhengtong, Jingtai and Tianshun periods of Ming dynasty witnessed social unrest and incessant foreign aggression and internal dissension, which led porcelain manufacture into a state of relaxation and slackness. At that time, imperial kiln porcelain with the reign titles of the three emperors could hardly be found; for this reason, the ceramic circle once held there was no porcelain production at that time and thus called this period "blank period". However, according to literature record and the incessant discovery of archaeological materials, there was porcelain manufacture during this period, though the number was indeed limited. As a ceramic of that period, *Blue-and-white dish with design of dragon among herbs* (No.24) collected by Guizhou Provincial Museum was particularly precious.

Shiny red glazed porcelain, widespread in China, is a popular collection of museums across the country. Yet, *Dark-red glazed bowl* (No.49) of Kangxi period, Qing dynasty, in imitation of Xuande collected by Guizhou Provincial Museum is indeed a rare treasure of this kind. Since Jiajing period of Ming dynasty, this kind was lost in transmission for nearly 200 years. It wasn't until Kangxi period that this kind revived. Shiny red glazed porcelain features crimson color, looking like red glow in clear sky after heavy storm. The thick glaze is densely covered with tiny pinholes, looking like orange peel; whereas the thin glaze is quite smooth and has no orange peel grain. *Dark-red glazed bowl* of Kangxi period collected by Guizhou Provincial Museum embodies not merely the common features of shiny red porcelain bowl of Kangxi period in imitation of the same kind of Ming dynasty, but also has its own distinctive features, representing the achievement of this kind in that period.

There are more examples: Eastern Jin *Celadon-glazed jar with appliqués of lotus petals* (No.3) boasts elegant modeling and exquisite carving. The exuberant lotus petals are so vivid that they are like the real blooming flowers, arousing people's tender affection. Southern Song bowls, cups, and plates of the Longquan kiln (No.16~19), comparable to sapphire and emerald, can lead you into an appreciation of the tranquility and purity of top grade celadon-glazed porcelain. The peculiar *Bowl with underglaze design of leaves* of the Jizhou kiln in Song dynasty (No.11), with leaves at the porcelain base, looks tender, beautiful and natural, and could be called a masterpiece of Jizhou kiln. *Cowpea-red glazed vase* (*Meirenzui*) *in the shape of willow leaf* (No.54), the rare collection during Kangxi period, looks delicate, exquisite and fair. The small green spots among the entire red looks tender and pleasing, arousing endless yearning and showing the mystery beauty of "moss spots among peach flowers and spring waves".

As is said, porcelain owns the beauty of blossoming flowers. Appreciating such brilliant ceramics of plentiful types, you will surely gain an enjoyment of beauty.

Guizhou Provincial Museum Tang Yan

图版目录

CONTENTS

图 版
PLATES

1

青瓷罐　高25.4cm，口径11.9cm，腹径24cm，底径17.2cm　东汉永元十六年（104年）

Celadon-glazed Jar

Height 25.4cm

Diameter of mouth 11.9cm

Diameter at the widest part of belly 24cm

Diameter of base 17.2cm

Sixteenth year of Yongyuan period of Eastern Han dynasty （104）

2

青瓷虎子　高17.7cm，长23cm，口径6cm　西晋

Celadon-glazed Vessel（*Huzi*）

Height 17.7cm

Length 23cm

Diameter of mouth 6cm

Western Jin dynasty

3

青釉堆塑莲瓣纹罐　高20.5cm，口径14cm，腹径22.2cm，底径15cm　东晋

Celadon-glazed Jar with Appliqués of Lotus Petals

Height 20.5cm

Diameter of mouth 14cm

Diameter at the widest part of belly 22.2cm

Diameter of base 15cm

Eastern Jin dynasty

4

青瓷四系罐　高8.6cm，口径7.7cm，底径7.5cm　东晋

Celadon-glazed Jar with four Handles

Height 8.6cm

Diameter of mouth 7.7cm

Diameter of base 7.5cm

Eastern Jin dynasty

5

青瓷蛙形水注　高4.5cm，口径2cm，底径5.7cm　六朝

Celadon-glazed Water Pot（*Shuizhu*）with Appliqués of Frog Head and Legs

Height 4.5cm

Diameter of mouth 2cm

Diameter of base 5.7cm

Six dynasties

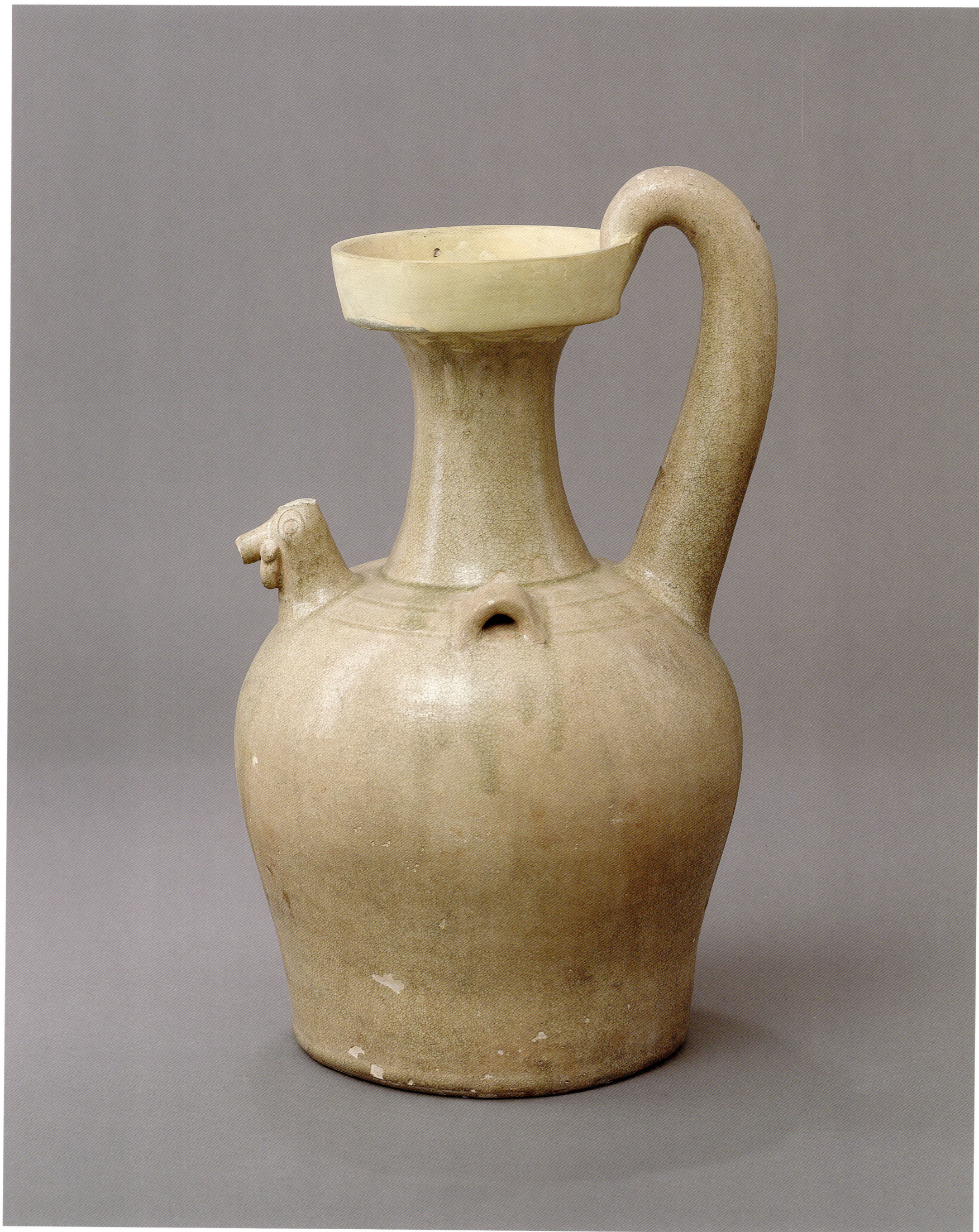

6（左）

青瓷鸡首壶　　通高44.8cm，口径2.5cm，底径19.3cm　　六朝

Celadon-glazed Chicken Head Ewer

Overall height 44.8cm

Diameter of mouth 2.5cm

Diameter of base 19.3cm

Six dynasties

7（上）

青瓷四系带盖罐　　通高8.4cm，腹径12.8cm，底径7cm　　南北朝

Celadon-glazed Covered Jar with four Handles

Overall height 8.4cm

Diameter at the widest part of belly 12.8cm

Diameter of base 7cm

Northern and Southern dynasties

8

青釉双龙耳瓶　高36.8cm，口径9cm，底径9.5cm　唐

Celadon-glazed Vase with two Dragon-shaped Handles

Height 36.8cm

Diameter of mouth 9cm

Diameter of base 9.5cm

Tang dynasty

9

白釉珍珠地缠枝花卉纹瓷枕　高8cm，长14cm，宽23cm　北宋

White-glazed Pillow with Design of Scrolled Flowers on Stamped Ring Ground

Height 8cm

Length 14cm

Width 23cm

Northern Song dynasty

10

建阳窑乌金釉兔毫盏　高5.4cm，口径10.85cm，底径3.1cm　宋
Golden-black Glazed Cup with Hare's Fur Effect（Jianyang kiln）
Height 5.4cm
Diameter of mouth 10.85cm
Diameter of base 3.1cm
Song dynasty

11

吉州窑叶片纹碗　高5.9cm，口径15.1cm，底径3.7cm　宋

Bowl with Underglaze Design of Leaves（Jizhou kiln）

Height 5.9cm

Diameter of mouth 15.1cm

Diameter of base 3.7cm

Song dynasty

12

吉州窑折枝花盏　高5.3cm，口径11cm，底径3.8cm　宋
Bowl with Underglaze Design of Flowers on the Inside（Jizhou kiln）
Height 5.3cm
Diameter of mouth 11cm
Diameter of base 3.8cm
Song dynasty

13

白釉黑牡丹纹瓷枕　高15cm，长20cm，宽14cm　宋

White-glazed Pillow with Overglaze Black Design of Ponies

Height 15cm

Length 20cm

Width 14cm

Song dynasty

14

影青皈依罐　高89.4cm，口径9.6cm，底径12.7cm　宋
Shadowy-blue Glazed Mortuary Jar with Appliqués of Figures
Height 89.4cm
Diameter of mouth 9.6cm
Diameter of base 12.7cm
Song dynasty

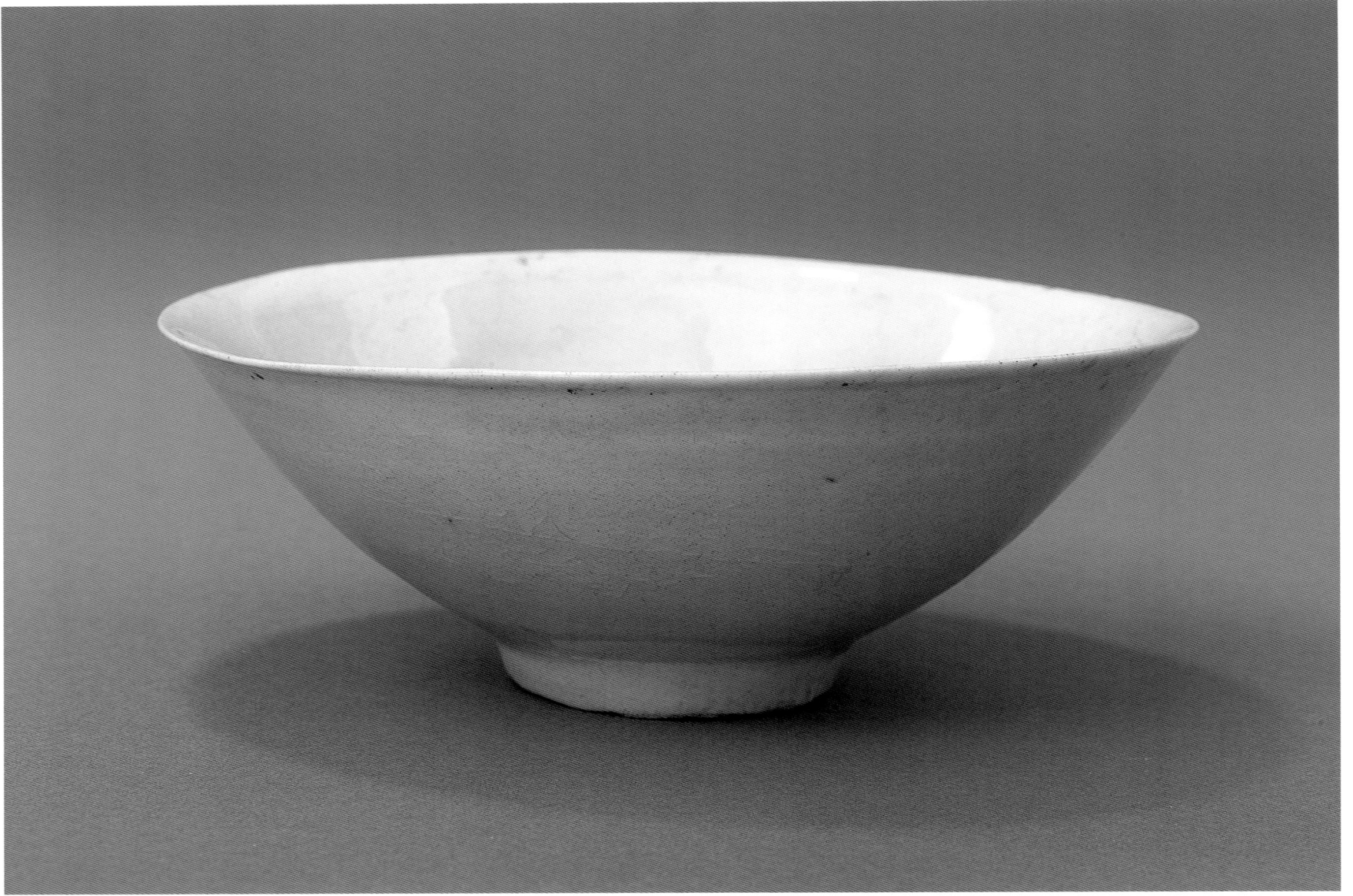

15

影青划花碗　高7.5cm，口径19.1cm，底径6cm　宋

Shadowy-blue Glazed Bowl with Incised Design of Flowers

Height 7.5cm

Diameter of mouth 19.1cm

Diameter of base 6cm

Song dynasty

16

龙泉窑笠式碗　高4.3cm，口径12.3cm，底径3.2cm　南宋

Bowl in the Shape of a Straw Hat（Longquan kiln）

Height 4.3cm

Diameter of mouth 12.3cm

Diameter of base 3.2cm

Southern Song dynasty

17

龙泉窑菊瓣纹杯　高4.6cm，口径8.8cm，底径3cm　南宋
Cup with Carved Design of Chrysanthemum Petals（Longquan kiln）
Height 4.6cm
Diameter of mouth 8.8cm
Diameter of base 3cm
Southern Song dynasty

18

龙泉窑双鱼纹盘　高4cm，口径13.6cm，底径6.1cm　南宋

Chrysanthemum-shaped Dish with Appliqués of Double Fish Inside（Longquan kiln）

Height 4cm

Diameter of mouth 13.6cm

Diameter of base 6.1cm

Southern Song dynasty

19

龙泉窑菊瓣纹盘　高3.2cm，口外径12.2cm，底径5.3cm　南宋
Dish with Carved Design of Chrysanthemum Petals（Longquan kiln）
Height 3.2cm
Diameter of mouth 12.2cm
Diameter of base 5.3cm
Southern Song dynasty

20

耀州窑青釉三足炉　高11.9cm，口径12cm，底径12.5cm　金

Celadon-glazed Tripod Incense Burner（Yaozhou kiln）

Height 11.9cm

Diameter of mouth 12cm

Diameter of base 12.5cm

Jin dynasty

21

青花什锦团花碗　高10cm，口径15.2cm，底径7.9cm　明宣德

Blue-and-white Bowl with Design of Flowers

Height 10cm

Diameter of mouth 15.2cm

Diameter of base 7.9cm

Xuande period of Ming dynasty

22

青花"福"字碗　高6.2cm，口径14.8cm，底径6.3cm　明正统

Blue-and-white Bowl with Inscription "*fu*（implying good fortune）"

Height 6.2cm

Diameter of mouth 14.8cm

Diameter of base 6.3cm

Zhengtong period of Ming dynasty

23

青花"福"字碗　高7cm，口径15cm，底径6cm　明正统

Blue-and-white Bowl with Inscription "*fu*（implying good fortune）"

Height 7cm

Diameter of mouth 15cm

Diameter of base 6cm

Zhengtong period of Ming dynasty

24

青花香草龙纹盘　高4cm，口径26.3cm，底径15.7cm　明天顺

Blue-and-white Dish with Design of Dragon among Herbs

Height 4cm

Diameter of mouth 26.3cm

Diameter of base 15.7cm

Tianshun period of Ming dynasty

27（左）

青花盖罐　通高15.1cm，口径5cm，底径6.3cm　明

Blue-and-white Covered Jar

Overall height 15.1cm

Diameter of mouth 5cm

Diameter of base 6.3cm

Ming dynasty

28（上）

白釉大瓷盘　高6.2cm，口径33.5cm，底径22.3cm　明嘉靖

White-glazed Dish

Height 6.2cm

Diameter of mouth 33.5cm

Diameter of base 22.3cm

Jiajing period of Ming dynasty

31

白釉隐刻双龙戏珠瓷杯 高4.4cm，口径9cm，底径3.1cm 明嘉靖

White-glazed Cup with Finely Incised Design of two Dragons Pursing a Fiery Orb

Height 4.4cm

Diameter of mouth 9cm

Diameter of base 3.1cm

Jiajing period of Ming dynasty

32

青花小瓶（一对）　高11.9cm，口径4.4cm，底径3.7cm　明万历

Pair of Blue-and-white Vases

Height 11.9cm

Diameter of mouth 4.4cm

Diameter of base 3.7cm

Wanli period of Ming dynasty

33

"黔府" 青花缠枝番莲盖罐　通高53.5cm，口径22.7cm，底径24cm　明万历

Blue-and-white Covered Jar with Design of Scrolled Passion-flowers, and the

Inscription "made in Year Dinghai，Wanli period，for Qian Mansion" on the Base

Overall height 53.5cm

Diameter of mouth 22.7cm

Diameter of base 24cm

Wanli period of Ming dynasty

34

青花瓜果纹罐　高18cm，口径8.8cm，底径12.8cm　明万历

Blue-and-white Jar with Design of Melons and Fruits

Height 18cm

Diameter of mouth 8.8cm

Diameter of base 12.8cm

Wanli period of Ming dynasty

35

酱色釉梅花碗　高4.5cm，口径9.8cm，底径4.2cm　明

Soy-brown Glazed Bowl with Overglaze Design of Plum Blossoms

Height 4.5cm

Diameter of mouth 9.8cm

Diameter of base 4.2cm

Ming dynasty

36（左）

白釉接引佛像　高23.4cm　明

White-glazed Statue of Amitabha（*Jieyinfo*）

Height 23.4cm

Ming dynasty

37（上）

白釉薄胎酒杯　高2.9cm，口径6.7cm，底径2.3cm　明

Egg-shell Cup with White Glaze

Height 2.9cm

Diameter of mouth 6.7cm

Diameter of base 2.3cm

Ming dynasty

38

青花人物杯　高3.6cm，口径5.6cm，底径2.3cm　明

Blue-and-white Cup with Design of Figures

Height 3.6cm

Diameter of mouth 5.6cm

Diameter of base 2.3cm

Ming dynasty

39

青花丹凤朝阳碗（一对）　　高4.8cm，口径13.9cm，底径7cm　　明

Pair of Blue-and-white Bowls with Design of Phoenix Singing in the Morning Sun

Height 4.8cm

Diameter of mouth 13.9cm

Diameter of base 7cm

Ming dynasty

40

五彩菊花盖罐　通高10.3cm，口径4.7cm，底径5cm　清顺治

Covered Jar with Overglaze Polychrome Design of Chrysanthemums

Overall height 10.3cm

Diameter of mouth 4.7cm

Diameter of base 5cm

Shunzhi period of Qing dynasty

41

青花麒麟芭蕉罐　高24cm，口径8.5cm，底径13cm　清顺治

Blue-and-white Jar with Design of Unicorn（*Qilin*）and Plantain Leaves

Height 24cm

Diameter of mouth 8.5cm

Diameter of base 13cm

Shunzhi period of Qing dynasty

42（左）

青花狮子牡丹盖罐　通高52cm，口径20cm，腹径33cm，底径25.7cm　清康熙

Blue-and-white Covered Jar with Design of Lions and Ponies

Overall height 52cm

Diameter of mouth 20cm

Diameter at the widest part of belly 33cm

Diameter of base 25.7cm

Kangxi period of Qing dynasty

43（上）

青花缠枝葡萄碗　高5.5cm，口径17.6cm，底径6.2cm　清康熙

Blue-and-white Bowl with Design of Scrolled Grapes

Height 5.5cm

Diameter of mouth 17.6cm

Diameter of base 6.2cm

Kangxi period of Qing dynasty

44（左）

青花九凤花卉瓶　高44.8cm，口径11.5cm，底径12.8cm　清康熙

Blue-and-white Vase with Design of nine Phoenixes and Flowers

Height 44.8cm

Diameter of mouth 11.5cm

Diameter of base 12.8cm

Kangxi period of Qing dynasty

45（上）

豇豆红釉龙团花太白尊　高8.8cm，口径3.4cm，底径12.8cm　清康熙

Cowpea-red Glazed Wine Pot（*Taibaizun*）with Design of Dragons（*Kui*）and Scrolled Flowers

Height 8.8cm

Diameter of mouth 3.4cm

Diameter of base 12.8cm

Kangxi period of Qing dynasty

46

五彩携琴访友瓶　高19cm，口径6.4cm，底径5.8cm　清康熙

Vase with Overglaze Polychrome Design of a Lofty Scholar Visiting Fiends

with a Servant Carrying a *Guqin*

Height 19cm

Diameter of mouth 6.4cm

Diameter of base 5.8cm

Kangxi period of Qing dynasty

47

青花开光课子图盖罐　高19.5cm，口径10.5cm，底径12.7cm　清康熙

Blue-and-white Covered Jar with Design of a Lady Taking Care of Children

Height 19.5cm

Diameter of mouth 10.5cm

Diameter of base 12.7cm

Kangxi period of Qing dynasty

48

粉彩鱼藻缸　高19cm，口径22.5cm，底径11.7cm　清康熙
Famille-rose Fish Tank with Design of Fish and Waterweeds
Height 19cm
Diameter of mouth 22.5cm
Diameter of base 11.7cm
Kangxi period of Qing dynasty

49

霁红釉瓷碗　高9.2cm，口径19.2cm，底径7.8cm　清康熙

Dark-red Glazed Bowl

Height 9.2cm

Diameter of mouth 19.2cm

Diameter of base 7.8cm

Kangxi period of Qing dynasty

50（左）

青花山水人物笔筒　高15.2cm，口径12cm，底径12cm　清康熙

Blue-and-white Brush Pot with Design of Figures and Landscape

Height 15.2cm

Diameter of mouth 12cm

Diameter of base 12cm

Kangxi period of Qing dynasty

51（上）

青花龙凤云纹碗　高9.1cm，口径19cm，底径8.6cm　清康熙

Blue-and-white Bowl with Design of Dragons，Phoenixes and Clouds

Height 9.1cm

Diameter of mouth 19cm

Diameter of base 8.6cm

Kangxi period of Qing dynasty

52

青花五彩儿童戏灯瓷瓶　高16cm，口径7.5cm，底径8cm　清康熙

Blue-and-white Vase with Overglaze Polychrome Design of Children Playing with Lanterns

Height 16cm

Diameter of mouth 7.5cm

Diameter of base 8cm

Kangxi period of Qing dynasty

53（左）

青花人物盖罐　通高36.5cm，口径13.3cm，底径15cm　清康熙

Blue-and-white Covered Jar with Design of Figures

Overall height 36.5cm

Diameter of mouth 13.3cm

Diameter of base 15cm

Kangxi period of Qing dynasty

54（右）

美人醉柳叶瓶　高16.2cm，口径3.6cm，底径2.3cm　清康熙

Cowpea-red Glazed Vase（*Meirenzui*）in the Shape of Willow Leaf

Height 16.2cm

Diameter of mouth 3.6cm

Diameter of base 2.3cm

Kangxi period of Qing dynasty

55（左）

红釉观音尊　高32.5cm，口径8cm，底径10cm　清康熙

Red-glazed Vase（*Guanyinzun*）

Height 32.5cm

Diameter of mouth 8cm

Diameter of base 10cm

Kangxi period of Qing dynasty

56（上）

茶褐色釉开片碗　高7.4cm，口径18.4cm，底径9cm　清雍正

Dark-brown Glazed Bowl with Crackled Glaze

Height 7.4cm

Diameter of mouth 18.4cm

Diameter of base 9cm

Yongzheng period of Qing dynasty

57

仿哥窑开片炉　高7.9cm，口径9.5cm，底径9cm　清雍正

Incense Burner with Crackled Glaze in Imitation of Ge Kiln

Height 7.9cm

Diameter of mouth 9.5cm

Diameter of base 9cm

Yongzheng period of Qing dynasty

58

斗彩石榴团花碗　高7.6cm，口径15cm，底径7.4cm　清雍正

Bowl with Overglaze Contrasting Colors（*Doucai*）Design of Pomegranates and Scrolled Flowers

Height 7.6cm

Diameter of mouth 15cm

Diameter of base 7.4cm

Yongzheng period of Qing dynasty

59

霁红釉水盂　高7.7cm，口径4.8cm，底径3.9cm　清雍正

Dark-red Glazed Water Pot（*Yu*）

Height 7.7cm

Diameter of mouth 4.8cm

Diameter of base 3.9cm

Yongzheng period of Qing dynasty

60

斗彩荷莲碟　高2.3cm，口径10cm，底径6.1cm　清雍正

Dish with Overglaze Contrasting Colors（*Doucai*）Design of Lotus Scrolls

Height 2.3cm

Diameter of mouth 10cm

Diameter of base 6.1cm

Yongzheng period of Qing dynasty

61（左）

胭脂红釉葫芦瓶　高20cm，口径5.1cm，底径4.2cm　清雍正

Carmine-glazed Vase in the Shape of Gourd

Height 20cm

Diameter of mouth 5.1cm

Diameter of base 4.2cm

Yongzheng period of Qing dynasty

62（上）

五彩归渔图盘　高2.8cm，口径28.4cm，底径21cm　清雍正

Dish with Overglaze Polychrome Design of Returning from Fishing

Height 2.8cm

Diameter of mouth 28.4cm

Diameter of base 21cm

Yongzheng period of Qing dynasty

63

仿哥窑瓶　高12.3cm，口径7cm，底径6.5cm　清雍正

Vase in Imitation of Ge Kiln

Height 12.3cm

Diameter of mouth 7cm

Diameter of base 6.5cm

Yongzheng period of Qing dynasty

64

豇豆红鼻烟壶　高7.5cm，宽3.8cm　清乾隆

Cowpea-red Glazed Snuff Bottle

Height 7.5cm

Width 3.8cm

Qianlong period of Qing dynasty

65（左）

粉青釉凸花荷塘鹭蝠瓶　高38.7cm，口径13.9cm，底径11.5cm　清乾隆

Lavender Grey Glazed Vase with Relief Decoration of Lotuses，Bats and Herons

（implying good fortune and wealth）

Height 38.7cm

Diameter of mouth 13.9cm

Diameter of base 11.5cm

Qianlong period of Qing dynasty

66（上）

蓝釉仿漆雕万字团寿纹碗（一对）　高4.1cm，口径11.7cm，底径6.7cm　清乾隆

Pair of Blue-glazed Bowls with Incised Design of Swastika（Buddhist symbol）Alternating with

the Character "shou（longevity）"，in Imitation of Carved Lacquerware

Height 4.1cm

Diameter of mouth 11.7cm

Diameter of base 6.7cm

Qianlong period of Qing dynasty

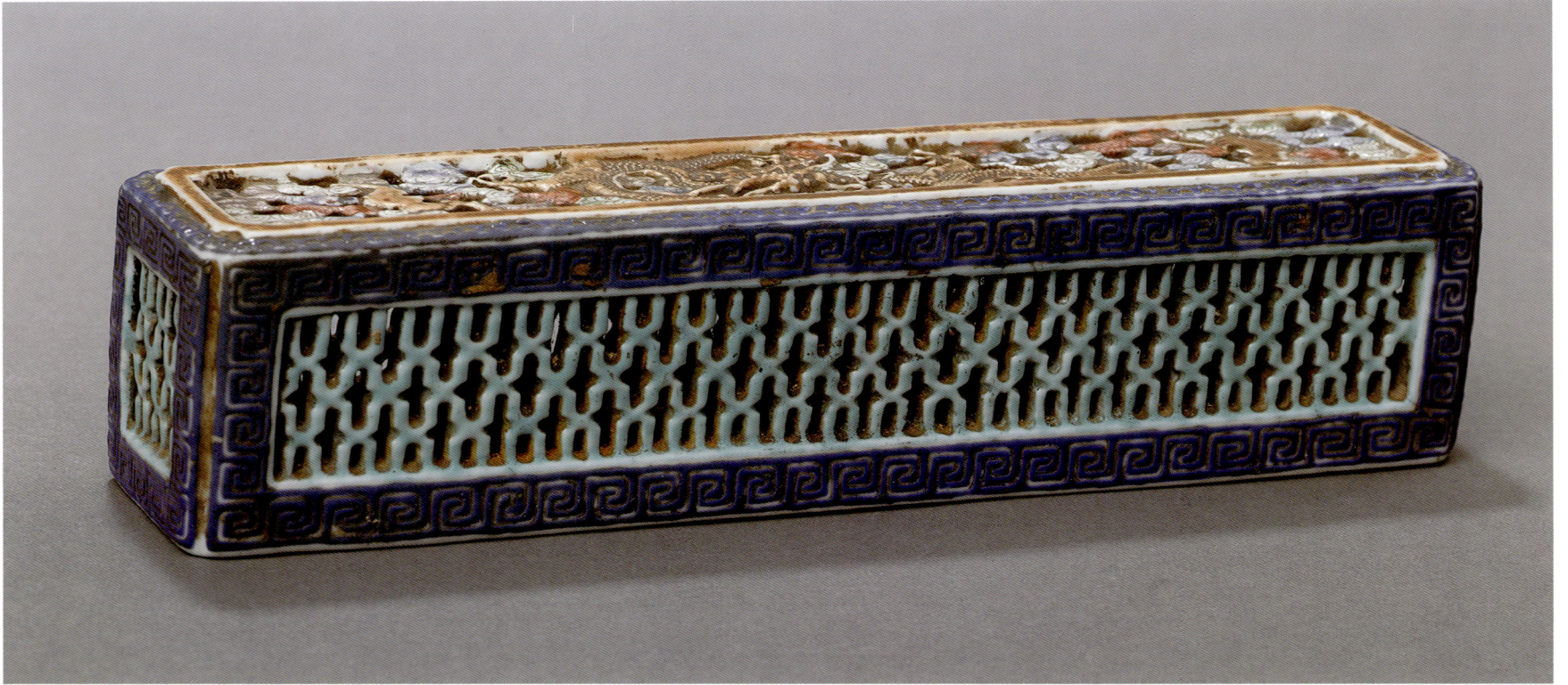

五彩贴金镂花云龙香盒　高4.5cm，长20.1cm，宽4.3cm　清乾隆

Openwork Incense Box with Overglaze Polychrome Design of Gold-foiled Dragons and Clouds

Height 4.5cm

Length 20.1cm

Width 4.3cm

Qianlong period of Qing dynasty

70

青花釉里红福禄寿纹汤碗　高9.1cm，口径21cm，底径8.1cm　清乾隆

Blue-and-white Soup Bowl with Underglaze Red Design of Bats，Deer and Pines

（implying good fortune，wealth and longevity）

Height 9.1cm

Diameter of mouth 21cm

Diameter of base 8.1cm

Qianlong period of Qing dynasty

71

斗彩五福缠枝碗（一对）　高6cm，口径13cm，底径4.9cm　清乾隆

Pair of Bowls with Overglaze Contrasting Colors（*Doucai*）Design of five Bats

（*Wufu*，implying good fortune），Flower Scrolls，and a "*daqing Qianlongnian*

zhi（made in Qianlong period）" Mark on the Base

Height 6cm

Diameter of mouth 13cm

Diameter of base 4.9cm

Qianlong period of Qing dynasty

72

硃砂红窑变釉瓶　高37.6cm，口径21.5cm，底径5cm　清乾隆

Vermilion Vase with Furnace Transmutation Glaze

Height 37.6cm

Diameter of mouth 21.5cm

Diameter of base 5cm

Qianlong period of Qing dynasty

73

青花缠枝番菊瓶　高17.1cm，口径5.5cm，底径6.5cm　清乾隆

Blue-and-white Vase with Design of Scrolled Passion-flowers

Height 17.1cm

Diameter of mouth 5.5cm

Diameter of base 6.5cm

Qianlong period of Qing dynasty

74

斗彩团菊纹盖罐　通高12.2cm，口径5.8cm，底径6.5cm　清乾隆

Covered Jar with Overglaze Contrasting Colors（*Doucai*）Design of Chrysanthemum Scrolls，and a "*daqing Qianlongnian zhi*（made in Qianlong period）" Mark on the Base

Overall height 12.2cm

Diameter of mouth 5.8cm

Diameter of base 6.5cm

Qianlong period of Qing dynasty

75

粉彩开光山水人物花卉瓷脸盆　高12.6cm，口径38cm，底径16cm　清乾隆至嘉庆

Famille-rose Washbasin with Design of Figures and Flower Scrolls

Height 12.6cm

Diameter of mouth 38cm

Diameter of base 16cm

Qianlong and Jiaqing periods of Qing dynasty

76（左）

青釉双鱼瓶　高24.7cm，口长4.4cm、宽2.7cm，底长9.5cm、宽7.4cm　清乾隆

Celadon-glazed Vase in the Shape of Double Fish

Height 24.7cm

Mouth：length 4.4cm，width 2.7cm

Base：length 9.5cm，width 7.4cm

Qianlong period of Qing dynasty

77（上）

青花缠枝莲带盖唾壶　通高5cm，口径4.5cm，底径8.4cm　清乾隆

Blue-and-white Covered Spittoon with Design of Scrolled Flowers

Overall height 5cm

Diameter of mouth 4.5cm

Diameter of base 8.4cm

Qianlong period of Qing dynasty

78

蓝釉描金菱口高足盘　高11.7cm，口径26.7cm，底径12cm　清乾隆

Blue-glazed Stem Dish with Overglaze Design of Flower Scrolls in Gold

Height 11.7cm

Diameter of mouth 26.7cm

Diameter of base 12cm

Qianlong period of Qing dynasty

79

青花荷莲碟　高1.8cm，口径7.8cm，底径6.2cm　清乾隆

Blue-and-white Dish with Design of Lotuses

Height 1.8cm

Diameter of mouth 7.8cm

Diameter of base 6.2cm

Qianlong period of Qing dynasty

80（上）

霁红釉盘　高4.6cm，口径20.8cm，底径13cm　清乾隆

Dark-red Glazed Dish

Height 4.6cm

Diameter of mouth 20.8cm

Diameter of base 13cm

Qianlong period of Qing dynasty

81（右）

什锦釉瓷瓶　高42cm，口径12.8cm，底径12cm　清乾隆

Multicolored-glazed Vase

Height 42cm

Diameter of mouth 12.8cm

Diameter of base 12cm

Qianlong period of Qing dynasty

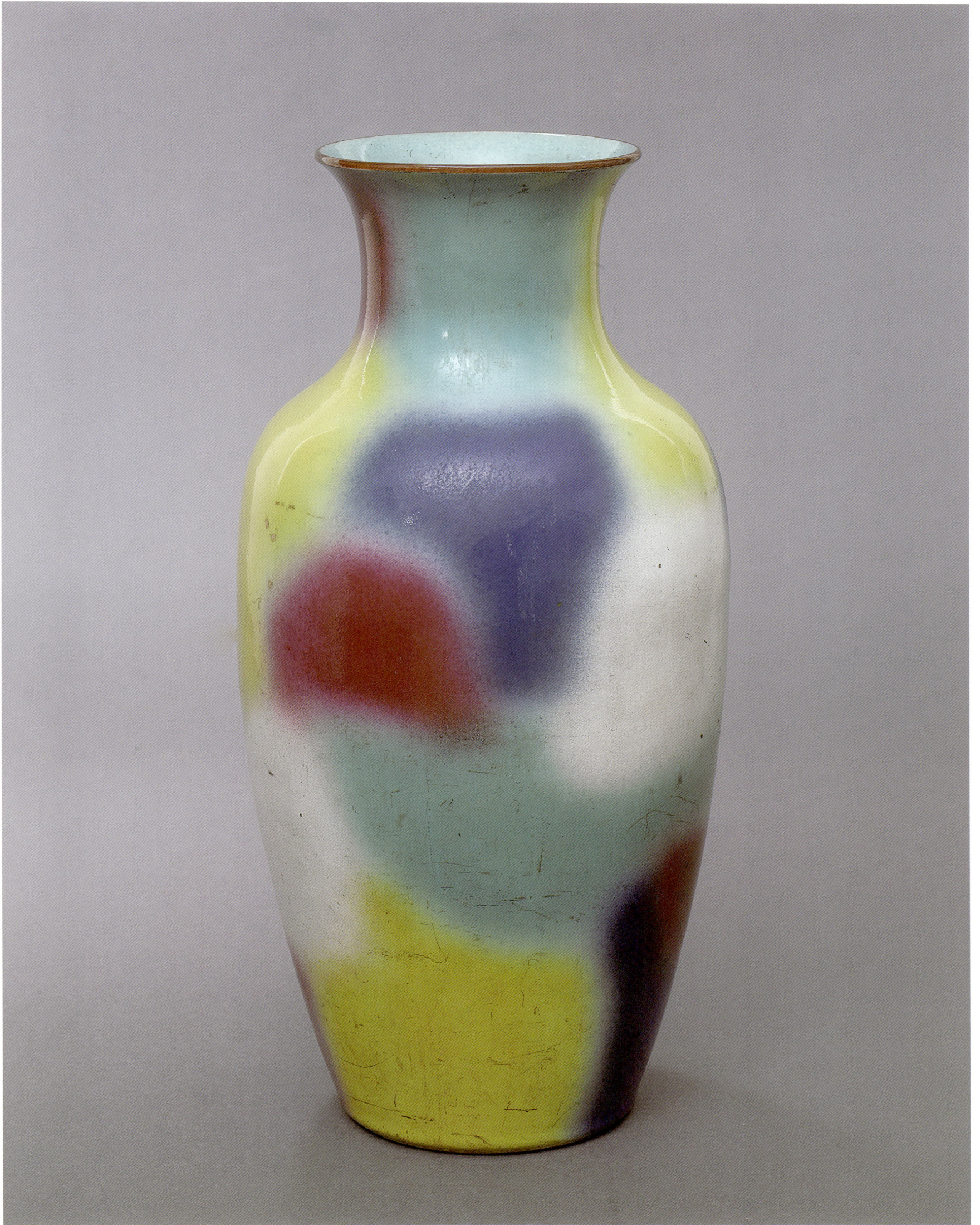

82（左）

青花缠枝莲纹壁挂瓶　高19cm，长7.2cm，宽4cm　清乾隆

Blue-and-white Hanging Vase with Design of Lotus Scrolls

Height 19cm

Length 7.2cm

Width 4cm

Qianlong period of Qing dynasty

83（上）

青花釉里红云龙纹瓷缸　高18cm，口径21.7cm，底径11.7cm　清乾隆

Blue-and-white Vat with Underglaze Red Design of Dragons and Clouds

Height 18cm

Diameter of mouth 21.7cm

Diameter of base 11.7cm

Qianlong period of Qing dynasty

84

芸豆红釉盘　高2.7cm，口径14.3cm，底径9cm　清乾隆

Kidney Bean Red Glazed Dish

Height 2.7cm

Diameter of mouth 14.3cm

Diameter of base 9cm

Qianlong period of Qing dynasty

85

青花荷塘鸳鸯碗　高7.3cm，口径16.3cm，底径9.8cm　清嘉庆

Blue-and-white Bowl with Design of Mandarin Ducks Swimming in a Lotus Pool,

and a "*daqing Jiaqingnian zhi*（made in Jiaqing period）" Mark on the Base

Height 7.3cm

Diameter of mouth 16.3cm

Diameter of base 9.8cm

Jiaqing period of Qing dynasty

86

青花釉里红松鹤花鸟瓶　高52cm，口径9.3cm，底径15.5cm　清嘉庆

Blue-and-white Vase with Underglaze Red Design of Deer，Cranes and Pines（meaning auspicious）

Height 52cm

Diameter of mouth 9.3cm

Diameter of base 15.5cm

Jiaqing period of Qing dynasty

87（左）

斗彩山水人物盖碗　通高6.8cm，口径6.7cm，底径2.7cm　清道光

Covered Bowl with Overglaze Contrasting Colors（*Doucai*）Design of
Figures and Landscape，and a "*chendingxuan*" Mark on the Base

Overall height 6.8cm

Diameter of mouth 6.7cm

Diameter of base 2.7cm

Daoguang period of Qing dynasty

88（上）

豆青釉矾红彩团凤纹碗　高6.8cm，口径14.3cm，底径6cm　清道光

Pea-green Glazed Bowl with Overglaze Design of Phoenixes

Height 6.8cm

Diameter of mouth 14.3cm

Diameter of base 6cm

Daoguang period of Qing dynasty

89

青花五彩龙凤碗（一对）　高6.4cm，口径14.8cm，足径5.8cm　清道光

Pair of Blue-and-white Bowls with Overglaze Polychrome Design of Dragons and Phoenixes

Height 6.4cm

Diameter of mouth 14.8cm

Diameter of base 5.8cm

Daoguang period of Qing dynasty

青花缠枝莲赏瓶　高39cm，口径9.7cm，底径13cm　清道光
Blue-and-white Vase with Design of Scrolled Passion-flowers
Height 39cm
Diameter of mouth 9.7cm
Diameter of base 13cm
Daoguang period of Qing dynasty

91

窑变釉石榴瓶　高18.5cm，口径10.5cm，底径8.6cm　清道光

Pomegranate-shaped Vase with Furnace Transmutation Glaze

Height 18.5cm

Diameter of mouth 10.5cm

Diameter of base 8.6cm

Daoguang period of Qing dynasty

92

霁蓝釉铁花如意耳瓶　高42cm，口径9cm，底径13.5cm　清道光

Blue-glazed Vase with Design of Paired *Ruyi*-shaped Handles on the Neck and Iron Appliqués

Height 42cm

Diameter of mouth 9cm

Diameter of base 13.5cm

Daoguang period of Qing dynasty

93

红釉敞口瓶　高36.6cm，口径14cm，底径14cm　清道光

Red-glazed Vase with a Flared Mouth

Height 36.6cm

Diameter of mouth 14cm

Diameter of base 14cm

Daoguang period of Qing dynasty

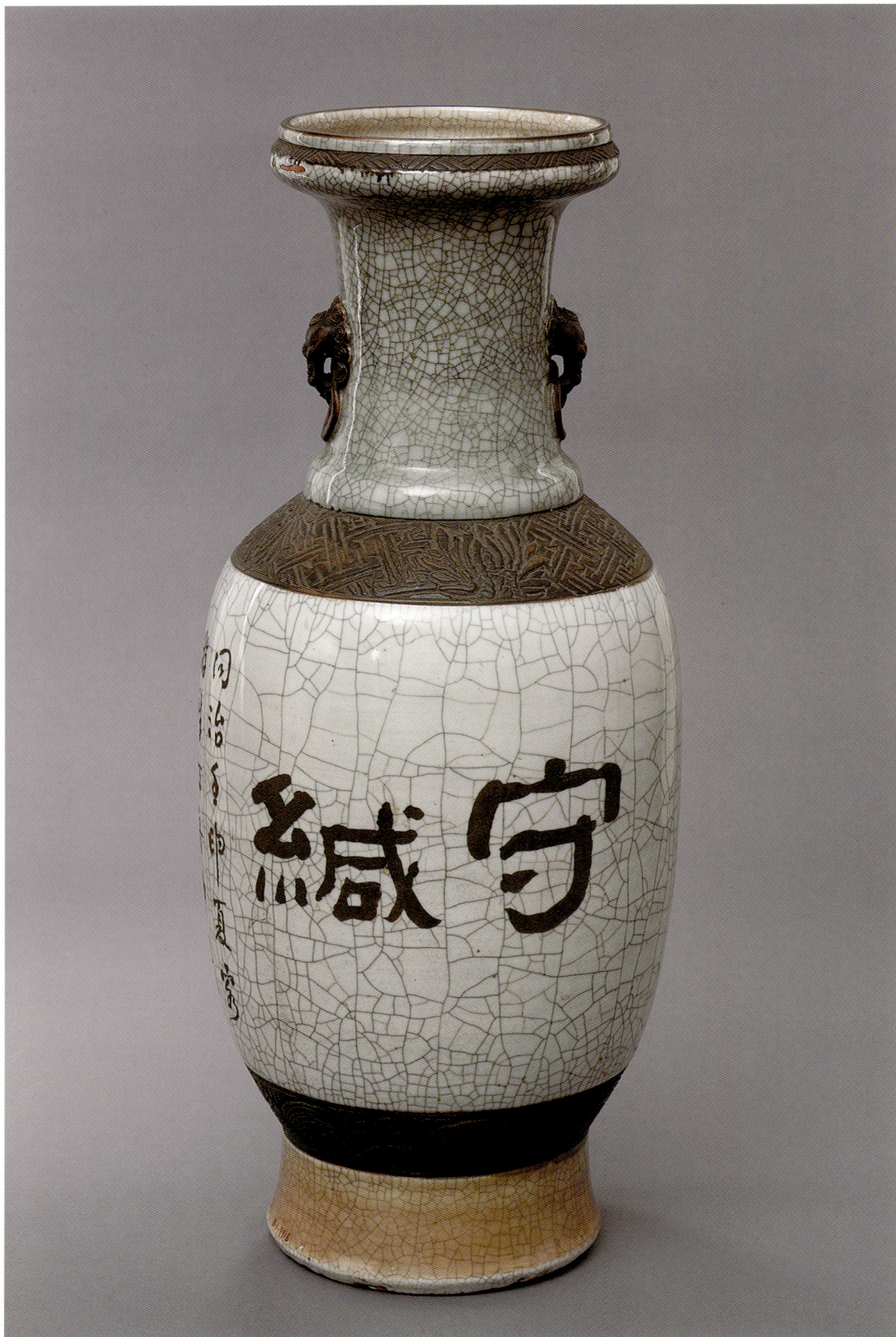

94

三色釉铁花兽耳衔环瓶　高60cm，口径16cm，底径17cm　清同治

Vase with Overglaze Characters "*shoujian*", and Iron Appliqués Including
Paired Beasts Holding a Hoop in the Mouth on the Neck

Height 60cm

Diameter of mouth 16cm

Diameter of base 17cm

Tongzhi period of Qing dynasty

95

青花卷草锦葵纹盖罐　通高17.5cm，口径14cm，底径10cm　清同治
Blue-and-white Covered Jar with Design of High Mallow Scrolls
Overall height 17.5cm
Diameter of mouth 14cm
Diameter of base 10cm
Tongzhi period of Qing dynasty

粉彩牡丹菊花碗（一对）　高8.5cm，口径17.3cm，底径7cm　清光绪

Pair of Famille-rose Bowls with Design of Ponies and Chrysanthemums

Height 8.5cm

Diameter of mouth 17.3cm

Diameter of base 7cm

Guangxu period of Qing dynasty

97（上）

藕荷色釉龙凤纹簠　高18cm，长25.4cm，宽20cm　清光绪

Pinkish-purple Glazed Grain Container（*Fu*）with Relief Decoration of
Dragons and Phoenixes

Height 18cm

Length 25.4cm

Width 20cm

Guangxu period of Qing dynasty

98（右）

茶叶末釉瓶　高32cm，口径7.3cm，底径15cm　清光绪

Tea-dust Glazed Vase

Height 32cm

Diameter of mouth 7.3cm

Diameter of base 15cm

Guangxu period of Qing dynasty

99

粉彩云蝠玉堂春瓶　高39cm，口径9.7cm，底径13cm　清光绪

Famille-rose *Yutangchun* Vase with Design of Bats and *Ruyi*-Shaped Clouds

Height 39cm

Diameter of mouth 9.7cm

Diameter of base 13cm

Guangxu period of Qing dynasty

100

霁蓝釉描金皮球花玉堂春瓶　高37cm，口径9.7cm，底径13cm　清光绪

Blue-glazed *Yutangchun* Vase with Overglaze Design of Round Flower Scrolls

Height 37cm

Diameter of mouth 9.7cm

Diameter of base 13cm

Guangxu period of Qing dynasty

101

"大雅斋"粉彩寿桃瓶　高75cm，口径24cm，底径24cm　清光绪

Famille-rose Vase with Overglaze Design of Peaches and a "*dayazhai*" Mark on the Neck

Height 75cm

Diameter of mouth 24cm

Diameter of base 24cm

Guangxu period of Qing dynasty

102（左）

茶叶末釉瓶　高32.7cm，口径7.3cm，底径15.2cm　清光绪

Tea-dust Glazed Vase

Height 32.7cm

Diameter of mouth 7.3cm

Diameter of base 15.2cm

Guangxu period of Qing dynasty

103（上）

蓝紫釉仿钧窑碗　高11.2cm，口径28cm，底径15.3cm　清光绪

Blue-violet Glazed Bowl in Imitation of Jun Kiln

Height 11.2cm

Diameter of mouth 28cm

Diameter of base 15.3cm

Guangxu period of Qing dynasty

青花龙纹盘　高4.8cm，口径34.2cm，底径20.2cm　清光绪

Blue-and-white Dish with Design of two Dragons Pursing a Fiery Orb

Height 4.8cm

Diameter of mouth 34.2cm

Diameter of base 20.2cm

Guangxu period of Qing dynasty

105

青花缠枝牡丹番菊敞口碗　高7.7cm，口径22.6cm，底径9.1cm　清

Blue-and-white Bowl with Design of Flower Scrolls

Height 7.7cm

Diameter of mouth 22.6cm

Diameter of base 9.1cm

Qing dynasty

106

仿哥窑水盂　高5.5cm，口径10.6cm，底径6.5cm　清

Water Pot（*Yu*）in Imitation of Ge Kiln

Height 5.5cm

Diameter of mouth 10.6cm

Diameter of base 6.5cm

Qing dynasty

107

白釉开片酱口水盂　高7.7cm，口径21cm，底径16.5cm　清

White-glazed Water Pot（*Yu*）with Crackled Glaze and Soy-brown Rim

Height 7.7cm

Diameter of mouth 21cm

Diameter of base 16.5cm

Qing dynasty

108（左）

窑变釉贯耳瓶　高29.8cm，口长10.5cm、宽9cm，底长11.7cm、宽9.1cm　清

Vermilion Vase with Furnace Transmutation Glaze and Paired Handles

Height 29.8cm

Mouth：length 10.5cm，width 9cm

Base：length 11.7cm，width 9.1cm

Qing dynasty

109（上）

白釉开片松鼠葡萄水盂　高6.2cm，口径18cm，底径15cm　清宣统

White-glazed Water Pot（*Yu*）with Crackled Glaze and Appliqués

of Squirrels and Grapes

Height 6.2cm

Diameter of mouth 18cm

Diameter of base 15cm

Xuantong period of Qing dynasty

图版说明

1

青瓷罐

高25.4cm，口径11.9cm，腹径24cm，底径17.2cm

东汉永元十六年（104年）

2

青瓷虎子

高17.7cm，长23cm，口径6cm

西晋

3

青釉堆塑莲瓣纹罐

高20.5cm，口径14cm，腹径22.2cm，底径15cm

东晋

4

青瓷四系罐

高8.6cm，口径7.7cm，底径7.5cm

东晋

5

青瓷蛙形水注

高4.5cm，口径2cm，底径5.7cm

六朝

6

青瓷鸡首壶

通高44.8cm，口径2.5cm，底径19.3cm

六朝

7

青瓷四系带盖罐

通高8.4cm，腹径12.8cm，底径7cm

南北朝

8

青釉双龙耳瓶

高36.8cm，口径9cm，底径9.5cm

唐

9

白釉珍珠地缠枝花卉纹瓷枕

高8cm，长14cm，宽23cm

北宋

10

建阳窑乌金釉兔毫盏

高5.4cm，口径10.85cm，底径3.1cm

宋

11

吉州窑叶片纹碗

高5.9cm，口径15.1cm，底径3.7cm

宋

12

吉州窑折枝花盏

高5.3cm，口径11cm，底径3.8cm

宋

13

白釉黑牡丹纹瓷枕

高15cm，长20cm，宽14cm

宋

14

影青皈依罐

高89.4cm，口径9.6cm，底径12.7cm

宋

15

影青划花碗

高7.5cm，口径19.1cm，底径6cm

宋

16

龙泉窑笠式碗

高4.3cm，口径12.3cm，底径3.2cm

南宋

17

龙泉窑菊瓣纹杯

高4.6cm，口径8.8cm，底径3cm

南宋

18

龙泉窑双鱼纹盘

高4cm，口径13.6cm，底径6.1cm

南宋

19

龙泉窑菊瓣纹盘

高3.2cm，口外径12.2cm，底径5.3cm

南宋

20

耀州窑青釉三足炉

高11.9cm，口径12cm，底径12.5cm

金

21

青花什锦团花碗

高10cm，口径15.2cm，底径7.9cm

明宣德

22

青花"福"字碗

高6.2cm，口径14.8cm，底径6.3cm

明正统

23

青花"福"字碗

高7cm，口径15cm，底径6cm

明正统

24
青花香草龙纹盘
高4cm，口径26.3cm，底径15.7cm
明天顺

25
青花碗
高5.8cm，口径12.8cm，底径5.8cm
明

26
青花坦口碗
高3.5cm，口径12.8cm，底径6cm
明

27
青花盖罐
通高15.1cm，口径5cm，底径6.3cm
明

28
白釉大瓷盘
高6.2cm，口径33.5cm，底径22.3cm
明嘉靖

29
鸡油黄隐龙纹盘
高6.2cm，口径36cm，底径15cm
明嘉靖

30
青花牡丹三狮纹碗
高5.6cm，口径11.1cm，底径4.8cm
明嘉靖

31
白釉隐刻双龙戏珠瓷杯
高4.4cm，口径9cm，底径3.1cm
明嘉靖

32
青花小瓶（一对）
高11.9cm，口径4.4cm，底径3.7cm
明万历

33
"黔府"青花缠枝番莲盖罐
通高53.5cm，口径22.7cm，底径24cm
明万历

34
青花瓜果纹罐
高18cm，口径8.8cm，底径12.8cm
明万历

35
酱色釉梅花碗
高4.5cm，口径9.8cm，底径4.2cm
明

36
白釉接引佛像
高23.4cm
明

37
白釉薄胎酒杯
高2.9cm，口径6.7cm，底径2.3cm
明

38
青花人物杯
高3.6cm，口径5.6cm，底径2.3cm
明

39
青花丹凤朝阳碗（一对）
高4.8cm，口径13.9cm，底径7cm
明

40
五彩菊花盖罐
通高10.3cm，口径4.7cm，底径5cm
清顺治

41
青花麒麟芭蕉罐
高24cm，口径8.5cm，底径13cm
清顺治

42

青花狮子牡丹盖罐

通高52cm，口径20cm，腹径33cm，底径25.7cm

清康熙

43

青花缠枝葡萄碗

高5.5cm，口径17.6cm，底径6.2cm

清康熙

44

青花九凤花卉瓶

高44.8cm，口径11.5cm，底径12.8cm

清康熙

45

豇豆红夔龙团花太白尊

高8.8cm，口径3.4cm，底径12.8cm

清康熙

46

五彩携琴访友瓶

高19cm，口径6.4cm，底径5.8cm

清康熙

47

青花开光课子图盖罐

高19.5cm，口径10.5cm，底径12.7cm

清康熙

48

粉彩鱼藻缸

高19cm，口径22.5cm，底径11.7cm

清康熙

49

霁红釉瓷碗

高9.2cm，口径19.2cm，底径7.8cm

清康熙

50

青花山水人物笔筒

高15.2cm，口径12cm，底径12cm

清康熙

51

青花龙凤云纹碗

高9.1cm，口径19cm，底径8.6cm

清康熙

52

青花五彩儿童戏灯瓷瓶

高16cm，口径7.5cm，底径8cm

清康熙

53

青花人物盖罐

通高36.5cm，口径13.3cm，底径15cm

清康熙

54

美人醉柳叶瓶

高16.2cm，口径3.6cm，底径2.3cm

清康熙

55

红釉观音尊

高32.5cm，口径8cm，底径10cm

清康熙

56

茶褐色釉开片碗

高7.4cm，口径18.4cm，底径9cm

清雍正

57

仿哥窑开片炉

高7.9cm，口径9.5cm，底径9cm

清雍正

58

斗彩石榴团花碗

高7.6cm，口径15cm，底径7.4cm

清雍正

59

霁红釉水盂

高7.7cm，口径4.8cm，底径3.9cm

清雍正

60

斗彩荷莲碟

高2.3cm，口径10cm，底径6.1cm

清雍正

61

胭脂红釉葫芦瓶

高20cm，口径5.1cm，底径4.2cm

清雍正

62

五彩归渔图盘

高2.8cm，口径28.4cm，底径21cm

清雍正

63

仿哥窑瓶

高12.3cm，口径7cm，底径6.5cm

清雍正

64

豇豆红鼻烟壶

高7.5cm，宽3.8cm

清乾隆

65

粉青釉凸花荷塘鹭蝠瓶

高38.7cm，口径13.9cm，底径11.5cm

清乾隆

66

蓝釉仿漆雕万字团寿纹碗（一对）

高4.1cm，口径11.7cm，底径6.7cm

清乾隆

67

五彩贴金镂花云龙香盒

高4.5cm，长20.1cm，宽4.3cm

清乾隆

68

粉彩如意蕃莲瓷盘

高2.5cm，口径14.7cm，底径9.1cm

清乾隆

69

黄地绿龙龙凤呈祥碗（一对）

高6.2cm，口径11.8cm，底径4.4cm

清乾隆

70

青花釉里红福禄寿纹汤碗

高9.1cm，口径21cm，底径8.1cm

清乾隆

71

斗彩五福缠枝碗（一对）

高6cm，口径13cm，底径4.9cm

清乾隆

72

硃砂红窑变釉瓶

高37.6cm，口径21.5cm，底径5cm

清乾隆

73

青花缠枝番菊瓶

高17.1cm，口径5.5cm，底径6.5cm

清乾隆

74

斗彩团菊纹盖罐

通高12.2cm，口径5.8cm，底径6.5cm

清乾隆

75

粉彩开光山水人物花卉瓷脸盆

高12.6cm，口径38cm，底径16cm

清乾隆至嘉庆

76

青釉双鱼瓶

高24.7cm，口长4.4cm、宽2.7cm，足长9.5cm、宽7.4cm

清乾隆

77

青花缠枝莲带盖唾壶

通高5cm，口径4.5cm，底径8.4cm

清乾隆

78

蓝釉描金菱口高足盘

高11.7cm，口径26.7cm，底径12cm

清乾隆

79

青花荷莲碟

高1.8cm，口径7.8cm，底径6.2cm

清乾隆

80

霁红釉盘

高4.6cm，口径20.8cm，底径13cm

清乾隆

81

什锦釉瓷瓶

高42cm，口径12.8cm，底径12cm

清乾隆

82

青花缠枝莲纹壁挂瓶

高19cm，长7.2cm，宽4cm

清乾隆

83

青花釉里红云龙纹瓷缸

高18cm，口径21.7cm，底径11.7cm

清乾隆

84

芸豆红釉盘

高2.7cm，口径14.3cm，底径9cm

清乾隆

85

青花荷塘鸳鸯碗

高7.3cm，口径16.3cm，底径9.8cm

清嘉庆

86

青花釉里红松鹤花鸟瓶

高52cm，口径9.3cm，底径15.5cm

清嘉庆

87

斗彩山水人物盖碗

通高6.8cm，口径6.7cm，底径2.7cm

清道光

88

豆青釉矾红彩团凤纹碗

高6.8cm，口径14.3cm，底径6cm

清道光

89

青花五彩龙凤碗（一对）

高6.4cm，口径14.8cm，底径5.8cm

清道光

90

青花缠枝莲赏瓶

高39cm，口径9.7cm，底径13cm

清道光

91

窑变釉石榴瓶

高18.5cm，口径10.5cm，底径8.6cm

清道光

92

霁蓝釉铁花如意耳瓶

高42cm，口径9cm，底径13.5cm

清道光

93

红釉敞口瓶

高36.6cm，口径14cm，底径14cm

清道光

94

三色釉铁花兽耳衔环瓶

高60cm，口径16cm，底径17cm

清同治

95

青花卷草锦葵纹盖罐

通高17.5cm，口径14cm，底径10cm

清同治

96

粉彩牡丹菊花碗（一对）

高8.5cm，口径17.3cm，底径7cm

清光绪

97

藕荷色釉龙凤纹簋

高18cm，长25.4cm，宽20cm

清光绪

98

茶叶末釉瓶

高32cm，口径7.3cm，底径15cm

清光绪

99

粉彩云蝠玉堂春瓶

高39cm，口径9.7cm，底径13cm

清光绪

100

霁蓝釉描金皮球花玉堂春瓶

高37cm，口径9.7cm，底径13cm

清光绪

101

"大雅斋"粉彩寿桃瓶

高75cm，口径24cm，底径24cm

清光绪

102

茶叶末釉瓶

高32.7cm，口径7.3cm，底径15.2cm

清光绪

103

蓝紫釉仿钧窑碗

高11.2cm，口径28cm，底径15.3cm

清光绪

104

青花龙纹盘

高4.8cm，口径34.2cm，底径20.2cm

清光绪

105

青花缠枝牡丹番菊敞口碗

高7.7cm，口径22.6cm，底径9.1cm

清

106

仿哥窑水盂

高5.5cm，口径10.6cm，底径6.5cm

清

107

白釉开片酱口水盂

高7.7cm，口径21cm，底径16.5cm

清

108

窑变釉贯耳瓶

高29.8cm，口长10.5cm、宽9cm，底长11.7cm、宽9.1cm

清

109

白釉开片松鼠葡萄水盂

高6.2cm，口径18cm，底径15cm

清宣统